IT'S A GOD THING!!!

By

JANET DOLAK

IT'S A GOD THING!!

A book of poems inspired by God

Written by Janet Dolak

Illustrated by Jesse Stryker

ISBN # 978-0-9979310-0-6

TABLE OF CONTENTS

THE THORNS UPON HIS HEAD

They placed the thorns
Upon His head.
Then whipped Him, beat Him 'til He bled.

And then they nailed
Him to the cross.
He died there. Oh, His life was lost.

They took Him down
With saddened gloom
And laid Him in a brand new tomb.

For three long days
He laid alone,
Then angels came, rolled back the stone.

When deep within
A woman looked,
There was no body and she shook.

She turned to run
To get the guard,
But there He stood alive but marred.

He rose again
For our salvation.
He lives within us – His creation.

GLORIOUS HOME OF JESUS

Look out the window and see the sight.
Glorious home of Jesus.
Look through the clouds at the brilliant light.
Glorious home of Jesus.

Look at the trees.
Look at the streams.
Look at the home of Jesus.
Mountains so tall.
Valley so small.
Look at the home of Jesus.

Look at the playground He made for you.
Beautiful home of Jesus.
Look at the rivers, the streams you pass too.
Glorious home of Jesus.

Look at the stars.
Look at the sky.
Look at the home of Jesus.
Look at God's face,
Then you'll know why.
Look at the home of Jesus.

Look all around you, there's love in the air.
Glorious home of Jesus.
He takes your problems, you've nary a care.
Beautiful home of Jesus.

Look at the hope.
Look at the smiles.
Look at the love of Jesus.
Children abound
Singing their songs.
Look at the love of Jesus.

Look at the sunrise with gold, red and blue.
Beautiful home of Jesus.
Look at the green grass all covered with dew.
Glorious home of Jesus.

Flowers that bloom.
Birds in the air.
Look at the home of Jesus.
Fields gold with grain;
His Grace is there.
Glorious home of Jesus.

THE HANDS UPON THE WALL

The hands upon the wall;
They start out oh so small.
Then they grow big,
That is His wish.
The hands upon the wall.

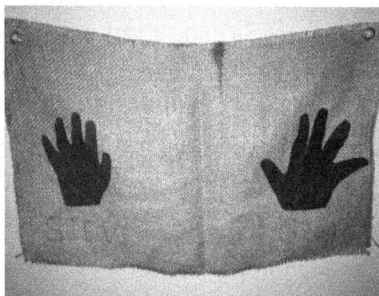

The hands show us the way;
They tell us what to say
By holding us,
By loving us.
The hands show us the way.

He loves us one and all.
We long to hear His call.
We love Him so.
In Him we grow,
And at His feet we fall.

We worship Him today.
We bow our heads and pray.
We talk to Him.
We walk with Him.
We worship Him His way.

He holds us in His arms.
He keeps us safe from harm.
We won't get lost,
He paid the cost.
Salvation is His charm.

And so by grace we're saved
From cradle to the grave.
We start out small
And then grow tall.
He guides us all our days.

GOD PAINTS US A PICTURE

When the sun sets in the west,
God paints us a picture.
He uses red and gold
And other colors too.
The beauty that we see
Is only just a sample
Of what God can do.

Beautiful lands.
Green grass in meadows.
Beautiful skies.
White clouds in blue.
Beautiful oceans
With large and small fishes.
These things were all made for you.

When day breaks in the east,
God paints us a picture.
He uses red and gold
And other colors too.
The beauty that we see
Is only just a sample
Of what God can do.

Mountains rise up.
Snow covers the caps.
Rivers run by;
They ripple away.
Bears, deer and squirrels
Are beasts that He gave us.
These things were all made for you.

When the sun is straight up,
God paints us a picture.
He uses blue and white
And other colors too.
The beauty that we see
Is only just a sample
Of what God can do.

Sunshine is warm,
Gentle rains are cooler.
Breezes kiss our face;
Tender as God's touch.
All things are good;
The earth and all that's in it.
He made all these things for you.

YOUR HELPING HAND

In the morning when I wake up
And there's darkness all around,
I look to you and wonder
As to how I'll get along.

You tell me not to worry,
That You'll send a helping hand.
And then the sun will come up
And I see glories with no end.

The sunlight helps me
And I know that You are there.
The sunlight helps me
And I know how much You care.

When I open up my cupboard
And I see that it is bare,
I look to You and wonder
Is there nothing left to share?

You tell me not to worry
That You'll send a helping hand.
And then my eyes will light up
And I see glories with no end.

For You sent manna
To the people in Your care.
For You sent manna
And I know that you are there.

When I walk out in Your meadows,
When I walk among the trees,
I hear the songbirds singing
And I fall down on my knees.

You tell me just to listen;
That You'll send an angel band,
And then the leaves will rustle,
There's much music in the land.

The birds are singing
And there's laughter in the air.
The birds are singing
And I hear glories everywhere.

When I lay down in the evening,
Your gentle touch I feel.
I sense that you are with me
And I know that You are real.

You tell me not to worry,
You'll protect me through the night.
My eyelids droop, I close them
And Your glories shine so bright.

And then I'm sleeping
And I'm cradled in Your arms.
And then I'm sleeping
And I know I'm free from harm.

DON'T BE ANGRY WITH ME, LORD

Don't be angry with me, Lord,
Just because I went astray.
Don't be angry with me, Lord,
I ask forgiveness on this day.

I'm so sorry, oh my Lord.
I know I hurt You when I sin.
It's hard to do what's right for You.
I need Your love. You let me win.

There's temptation all around
And it's so awfully hard to fight.
Your grace and love for us abound.
It's what I need to set me right.

Please forgive my weakness, Lord.
I tried so many times to turn.
I need Your strength to keep me strong,
Because for You I truly yearn.

A SEED IS PLANTED

A seed is planted.
The roots go down into the earth.
The green shoots so very small

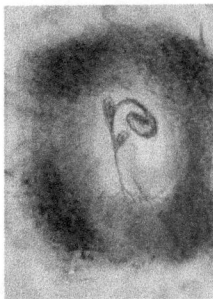

Come up to meet the sun.
It grows and sprouts leaves
Coming ever nearer to the warmth of the sun.
The rains fall down and quench the thirst.
The tender shoots grow strong in Your care.
As the shoots turn to plants
The leaves grow broad.
Then buds begin.
The sun and the rain, the warmth of the soil
Continue to care for the growth.
The buds grow stronger
And turn into flowers
Which slowly open and show Your beauty here on earth.

Another seed is planted.
The roots go down into the earth.
The green shoots so very small
Come up to meet the sun.
It grows and sprouts leaves
Coming ever nearer to the warmth of the sun.
The rains fall down and quench the thirst.
The tender shoots grow strong in Your care.
As the shoots turn to plants..
This one is different.
The stem grows strong
And becomes a sturdy stalk
Rising ever and ever closer to the sky.
Stronger it grows until the stalk becomes a trunk.
The trunk grows higher and higher
Adding branches, which reach
Out to the sun and rain.
The buds on this plant turn to
Leaves, which rustle in the wind
And provide shade.
Birds rest on the branches
And build homes among the foliage.
The tree bursts forth with Your beauty here on earth.

A third seed is planted.
This seed is different.
It grows inside of us.
As we hear Gods word of how He made Heaven and earth,
Its roots go down into the soil and take hold.
As we learn about Abraham, Moses and Noah,
The tender shoots break the surface and rise to meet the Son.
They grow ever taller and stronger warmed by the Son.
The Son and rain quench our hunger and thirst.
We hear the story of Jesus' birth
And the leaves begin to sprout.
In learning about Jesus' life and death
Gentle care continues for the tender growth.
The buds begin to develop and take shape.
When Jesus rose from the dead,
The flowers bloom and we reflect His beauty here on earth.

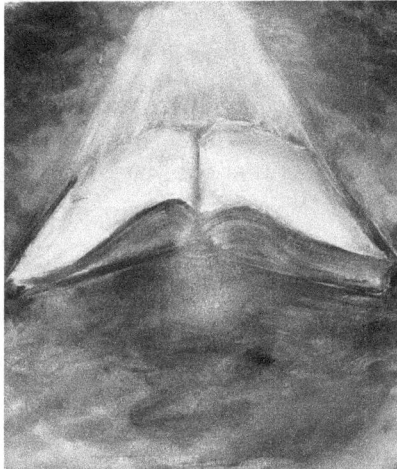

WHY SHOULD I TELL THEM ABOUT YOU?

Why should I tell them about You?
Why should I mention Your name?
Because after I heard about You
My life was never the same.

What should I tell them about You?
Should I tell them the tale of Your birth?
How cows shared their manger with You?
And three wise men came carrying myrrh.

Should I tell them how a king tried to kill You?
While You were still only a child?
How You asked priests difficult questions?
How Your manner was tender and mild?

What miracles should I mention about You?
How you walked on the waters at sea?
Water turned to wine at the wedding.
How all of this impressed even me?

And then should I tell them about You?
How You made lots of sick people well?
And how You loved the small children.
It's such a great story to tell.

Should I tell them what men said about You?
That Your life was heavenly made?
But some men were envious of You.
They hated the joys that You gave.

I know I must tell them about You.
When You rode in the city that day.
Hail to the King! Alleluia!
With palm branches lining Your way.

But I also must tell them about You
And of Judas's betrayal that day.
How the soldiers came to arrest You,
And violently took You away.

And this part I must tell about You
How nailed to the cross You forgave.
You cried out, "Now it is over!"
And forever in heaven we'll live.

There's no question I must tell them about You.
That in three days You rose from the grave.
And that these things all happened to You
So that all of mankind could be saved.

I must tell them these things about You.
So belief in You they can choose too.
For there's only one doorway to heaven,
And that doorway is centered on You.

WHAT WILL IT BE LIKE?

I sit alone in the company of my Lord.
This is when my Spirits always soar.
He's all I need to keep me feeling free.
I sit at the foot of my most precious Jesus.

When I sit alone with
Silence all about,
I look up at the sky and wonder what?

What will it be like?
When I go on up to heaven?
What will it be like?
When I see Jesus face to face?
What will it be like?

Will I fall down on my knees?
Will I be speechless if you please?
Will I join the angel choir?
Or will I just admire
The beauty and the brilliance of His face?

What will it be like
In that longed for distant place?

On earth we feel the warming glow of the sun.
On earth gentle breezes caress our face.
On earth we splash in the waters of oceans.
On earth we see trees and flowers and bushes.
But what will it be like
When I go on up to heaven?

Will there be crowds bustling about?
Will there be time enough to shout,
Glory to the Lord!
How could we ever get bored?
Will we sing praises to our King?
Is there a dinner bell to ring?
Or will we just hear strings of angel's harps?

On earth we always scurry.
We're always in a hurry.
We've tasks we must complete,
And friends we want to meet.
The furniture needs dusting;
The pipes – oh no – they're rusting!
The lawn needs mowing,
The seeds we're sowing.
But what will it be like
When we go on up to heaven?

Will we have all the time there is?
To honor what is His?
We'll sing, we'll shout,
We'll run about.
We'll give him praise
Through all our days.
It will be grand.
I know it will,
When we go on up to Heaven.

A BIRD FLEW UP TO MY WINDOW TODAY

A bird flew up to my window today.
He cocked his head as if to say,
"Let me in, I'm cold.
Let me in, I'm lonely.
Let me in. I want to talk with you."

Then he sat on the sill and swayed
His feet held – an hour he stayed.

'Let me give you a message.
Let me tell you a tale.
Let me tell you about my dear friend.

"My friend dressed in robes and sandals.
He walked everywhere that He went
But then there were days,
And then there were nights
That my friend had no place to stay.

"I followed Him all around towns.
I sat on His shoulder for hours.
He loved little children,
He loves even you.
You weren't even born that is true.

"My friend made the blind man to see.
My friend made the lame boy to walk.
He turned water to wine.
Yes, He's divine.
The miracles my friend can do!!!

"Then one day some bad men came by.
They wanted my dear friend to die.
He didn't resist,
Did not run away.
He let them put nails through His wrists.

"The cross it rose up toward the sky.
He said, 'Not for Me should you cry.
I will be back.
I promise you that.'
His purpose He could not deny.

"I saw Him again don't you know.
Three days later I saw Him once more.
'Believe Me,' He said.
'I rose from the dead.
Your sins are as white as the snow.'"

And then the bird flew away.
I guess he had no more to say,
But just as he left
He gave me a gift.
His friend, don't you know is THE WAY.

AS I SIT

As I sit on this mountain top
The air is chilly but the sun warms my face.
I look out over the valley
And see the wonders of God's Grace.

As I sit beneath this tree
Whose arms protect me with its shade,
I look at the grass beneath me
And I see God's details in each blade.

As I sit upon this rock
Which is sturdy, smooth, and hard,
I look out over the field
And I see the awesome power of my Lord.

As I sit beside this lake
With gentle ripples lapping at the shore,
I look out over the water
And I see God's miracles galore.

As I sit up on this cloud
So light and fluffy, up so high,
I look around with awe
And I see all God's marvels from the sky.

IT'S A GOD THING!!!

When you wake up on time
But your alarm didn't ring;
When you don't feel like laughing
But are willing to sing;
When you're puzzled and wonder
Don't give it a thought,
The answer's quite simple
It's a God Thing.

When you search for an idea
And it was there all along;
When things suddenly go right
When before they went wrong;
Don't look any farther
An explanation to find,
It's really very simple
It's a God Thing.

When you're late for a meeting
And your boss is late too;
When you're meeting a stranger
But it's someone you knew;
The funny thing is
That it's sure meant to be
Just another example
Of a God Thing.

When your wallet is empty
And buying milk is a need;
You reach in your pocket
Five dollars indeed!
It didn't just grow there
It wasn't a trick,
It's a God Thing again!
So don't be so thick!!

When you think of an old friend
And he calls you that night;
Don't think it's just freaky
Please look at it right.
God planted the notion
In both of your minds
To talk to each other
Was another God Thing.

When you're determined
To do one thing or another,
But things don't go right
You might think "oh, brother!"
You really should be
Looking high up above
Because what just happened
Was a God Thing!

When you look at a sunset
And drink in the sight;
Or look at the sunrise
The day's starting out right;
The awesome feeling
That takes over you then
Can only be one thing,
It's a God Moment!

When you hold your first child
Or your grandchild so tender
For the first time or second
And your heart you surrender,
What stirs deep within you
Must come from on high.
It's nothing you did,
It's a God Moment!

When you need something badly
And you ask it in prayer.
If you receive it tomorrow
That wouldn't be so rare.
Don't think it is strange
A coincidence, "So There!"
Be assured that it's really
A God Thing!

SWEET PERFUME

I stand by my door
And I smell sweet perfume.
I look all around
And there's nothing in bloom.

I walk down the hallway.
I smell it there too.
The scent is so sweet
And the strength of it grew.

I drive down the side street
To go to my home.
Overwhelming is fragrance
I breathe in and moan.

I crawl 'neath my blankets
Some sleep to enjoy.
Again I smell Jesus.
He's with me! Oh, Boy!

I know it is Jesus,
It can be no other.
I smell a sweet smell
That around me still hovers.

There aren't any flowers;
No blossoms in sight
To fill up my senses
In daytime or night.

My Jesus is near me.
He tells me in ways
That man cannot muster.
His fragrance will stay.

ANGELS

I see shadows moving all about.
Just what they are, I have no doubt.
They flutter here, they flutter there.
They seem to flutter everywhere.

Some shapes are angels with two wings.
Some with harps: I hear them sing.
Some seem to change before my eyes.
Some shimmer. Truly – that's no lie!

They move about from place to place.
I never seem to see a face.
At times they sit so very still.
Each time I see them – what a thrill!

I close my eyes when they pass by.
They give me angel bumps. But, why?
Perhaps because their touch is gentle.
Perhaps I'm simply sentimental.

It doesn't matter what the reason.
It seems to happen every season.
They seem to show up more and more
Until they cover up the floor.

They come in twos and threes and fours.
They come through windows, walls and doors.
They form an army all around.
They're here to keep us safe and sound.

For God sends guardians from above.
He shows us just how much we're loved.
So even if you don't see any.
I'll tell you true that there are many!!

www.ingramcontent.com/pod-product-compliance
Lightning Source LLC
Chambersburg PA
CBHW060548030426

42337CB00021B/4499